Finding True Happiness

By Jane Steward

Published by
Steward Publications
751 Blackmoor Circle
Neenah, WI 54956

Printed by
Print Source Plus, Inc
1314 W. College Avenue
Appleton, WI 54914

Printed in the United States of America

ISBN: 978-145071804-2

Library of Congress Catalog Number: 2010907355

First Printing: June 2010

10 09 08 07 06 5 4 3 2 1

Contributions

I would like to thank my family and friends for being there when I needed them most. I love them all from the bottom of my heart, and hope to be there for them when they need me.

I would like to thank my psychotherapist, Char Groves, M.S., LMFT, for opening my eyes even when it hurt so bad I wanted to die.

I would like to thank Susan Robinson for helping me edit my book.

I would also like to thank my niece Stephanie Dauson for her artistic talent on the cover and back of my book.

I would like to also thank Nancy Miller for proofreading my book. And lastly I would like to thank my fiancé, Kevin Dolan, for helping me with my citings, and for all his love and support.

IMPORTANT NOTE: I used several wonderful references in writing this book. They are each identified by a number in brackets [1], so that you can tell where I found some of the source information that I used when writing this book. The full information about each source is at the end of this book.

Contents

Introduction

Do you believe that everyone has a purpose in life? Well, I do, and that's why I am writing this book.

All my life I have had to learn about life the hard way. Why do you think that is?

In school we learn about math, reading, and writing, but not about life in general. I graduated from high school in 1978. At that time, the only psychology class available was in high school. We have come a long way in schools by offering our students different types of counseling, but I would like to see some form of a pre-psychology classes offered earlier in our schools. A psychology class for children in each grade to expose our children to real life learning at an earlier age. Then and only then will we give ourselves and our children the knowledge and tools that are needed to help us deal with life's problems before it is too late. Whose child will be next to deal with sexual abuse, drug or alcohol abuse, or living in a home with codependency or depression that they don't understand? Health and technology keep getting more advanced, but people are still making the same mistakes; mistakes about ourselves, relationships, drugs, alcohol, and depression.

We are living in a very private and closed society these days. Our homes are closed to most outsiders. Because of this, many children are not exposed to what a "normal" household is like. We need to get them used to talking about themselves and their lives when they are very young. This way, if something does happen to them, they will know it is okay to talk about what is bothering them and we can take care of their needs.

In this book we will learn how to find true happiness for ourselves and for our children.

Chapter One: Finding Your Inner Child

The most beautiful thing my psychotherapist did for me was to help me find my inner child.

We are all children. The only difference is that now our dolls are babies, and the trucks we used to play with, now we drive.

Try to imagine what it was like when you were in your mother's womb (try to be in a quiet room where you feel comfortable). Think of how content you were – not a care in the world. Find and feel your inner peace.

Now think of when you were in your mother's arms, all wrapped up in a warm blanket, where no one has ever hurt you yet in any way. She smiles at you, and you smile back. Just feel the love between the two of you. Now try to remember when you were a little child, playing by yourself with your favorite toy. Look hard. Do you see him/her? That is your inner child. He/she is still there.

The inner child represents the innocent hope inside all of us, and the part of us that can still see the wonder in things.

Now take the time to write down what you think your relationship is with yourself.

_____

_____

_____

_____

_____

_____

If you have a good relationship with yourself, you will love yourself, believe in yourself, and you will find hope in your life. You will "light the flame inside your soul" [from *Playing It By Heart: Taking Care of Yourself No Matter What*, by Melody Beattie [1]] and take care of all your needs to be healthy, happy, and content.

The most important thing I learned in counseling is to pay attention to what you are feeling. Listen to and understand your feelings. Sit down and ask yourself, why am

I feeling this way? Then, do something about it. If something doesn't feel right, trust your instinct – your intuition. This includes your dreams. Below is an excerpt from *The Nightmare Encyclopedia* by Jeff Belanger and Kirsten Dalley [2]:

Dreams are the intuitions when we sleep. If we pay attention to our dreams, we can get to know ourselves better. It will help us decide what to do with our lives.

Dreams – the wandering soul – they are the language of our souls. The sights, sounds, and sensations we experience in our dreams speak directly to us and for us, while we're unconscious.

Nightmares, on the other hand, which may be based on real events, or subconscious nightmares, can be very hard to shake.

Precognitive dreams are a special case of extrasensory perception. In a precognitive dream (a dream that comes true), the dreamer experiences an event in whole or in part, before it will occur.

Recurring nightmares – having the same kind of nightmares over and over again. Recurring nightmares usually indicate that the dreamer is dealing with some unresolved issues that are "stuck" in the unconscious and making themselves known in the dreams. The issue may not be clear, and the simple repetition in the dream will probably not make the issue any clearer to the dreamer. These nightmares will continue until the individual is able to integrate the traumatic experience into his/her waking life. They may be telling you of a premonition – a forewarning. Something is not right in your life." [2]

Don't ever doubt yourself.

True happiness comes from inside you. You can often feel this happiness when you sit in a quite area with no TV, no music; only you, and if you like who you are, you will feel happiness and be content for the moment.

I remember going to work after my boyfriend (I will call him Jason) and I broke up after a long-term relationship, and one of my friends asked me how I could work and be happy. I said that's one thing he cannot take away from me is my happiness.

"No matter what happens in the world around you, no matter how people treat you, and no matter what your finances are, you still have yourself." (from "Want A Happier Life? Try This, A Gratitude Adjustment Is Simple Therapy," Contributing Editor M. J. Ryan, *Health* Magazine) [3]

You have to love and trust yourself before you can truly love and trust another person.

"Does your happiness depend on your circumstances, or your attitude?" [3]

Be positive about yourself. "At every moment you have a choice to look at what is

right or wrong with yourself and your life."
[3]

If you don't like who you are, work on it.
How? In the remaining chapters to come, we
will learn how to do just that.

Only then will you find true happiness in
your life.

Chapter Two: Why Do We Need God?

God is the only relationship we will ever have with us 24/7, until the day we die.

It is the most important relationship you will ever need. This relationship is your Faith, Spirit, Soul, and Forgiveness. For with God in your life, you will always be loved.

Did you ever feel you were alone? If you believe in God, Jesus, and angels, you will never be alone.

What would you do if someone took your child? You would pray to God, "Please bring my child back to me." You would call the police, put posters up around your neighborhood and notify the TV stations. You would have a search done. You would do whatever you could to find your child and bring them home safely.

When we have no control over something, we need to believe in God to keep us strong. This book would not be complete without this chapter, because God has made us who we are.

Before I go any further with this chapter, I would like to share with you why I believe in God. First, it was the way I was brought up; I am a Christian. The other reasons that I will always believe in God are as follows.

First of all, two years before my dad died, my parents and I had a dispute over where my son should live. I obviously wanted him to continue to live with me but they felt it would be best if he lived with them. In the end, he ended up living with my parents against my will. Because of this I didn't let my parents see my daughter or myself for two years for fear that they would try to take my daughter as well. The night before my dad died, my brother told me he was on his deathbed. So my brother, my daughter, and I went to the hospital to say our good-byes. I told my dad I loved him. All he said was, "Don't worry, I will be fine."

Later that night I was awaken by my dog who had started to bark at something in the other room. I looked at the clock (it was a little after 1:00 a.m.) and then got up to check on the dog. He was barking at the cat door that led to the basement. When I looked closer I saw that a bat was trying to get through the small cat door. I quickly taped it up and went back to bed. All this while my daughter was still sleeping upstairs. In the morning I went to my brother's house to ask him to help me find the bat that I had seen the night before. He said, "Jane, sit down. Dad passed away last night." He said the time. It was exactly the same time the bat was trying to get through the cat door. We never found the bat. I lived in that house for years and never saw a bat in the house.

I couldn't get it off my mind, so I talked to a psychotherapist about it, and she had thought that maybe my dad wanted to say good-bye. The bat was certainly not my dad. Ecclesiastes teaches us that our soul goes to God when we die, while our bodies remain here until the resurrection.

Then I read about bats in *The Nightmare Encyclopedia*. "Some say it may warn of death, or the ending of something important, such as an unresolved relationship." [2]

Maybe it was just a dream. The only thing I am sure of is the cat door was taped up when I woke up. Was I sleepwalking?

At my dad's funeral I felt so peaceful. All I could see was that bat. I didn't even cry. If I trust my instincts about what had happened, I do believe that somehow I was being told it's okay. I do have closure with my dad. I felt peace with him knowing that he did love me and wanted to say good-bye to my daughter and myself.

Another thing that reinforced my belief in God happened when I was with Jason, a man who I loved with all my heart. I realized after he left me that he was an alcoholic, a sex addict, and that he exhibited other abusive traits. I tried to get him to see a psychotherapist so he could get the help he needed and we could be a family again. He refused. So I prayed every night, crying myself to sleep, that he would get help and we could be a family again.

This went on for months. One night, I woke up and standing by my bed was a man with a white, round face, wearing a hooded black cloak. I even felt his presence. I covered my eyes with the palms of my hands for a few seconds, and when I pulled my hands away from my eyes, he was gone. That was the last time I ever prayed for him to get the help he needed and for us to get back together.

Was it a dream? Was it Jason? (He still had a key to the house, and it was around Halloween, so he might have been wearing a costume). I don't think so, because if he had gone through all that trouble, he would have done something to me, and why didn't I hear the door when he left? The only thing that makes sense to me is that God sent a cloaked figure (a sign of death) to me, saying, "Jason is not willing to get help, and if you ever take him back he will finish you off."

Unless you've ever experienced anything like these two occurrences it is very hard to comprehend, but God can manifest Himself to us in many ways. He could have his angels manifest themselves to us in any way, shape or form. To me, it was a wake-up call – not knowing how much danger my life was in. I will always believe someone is watching over me.

I can't speak for other religions; however, Christianity sets boundaries. We try to live by God's rules; otherwise whose rules would we live by? Would we make them up as we go? I do believe that many religions have about the same rules for living. So, for the most part, if we all live by God's rules we will live in harmony.

If we start teaching our children about God in a fun, kind, and loving way, not to push it on them or smother them with our teachings, we will feel the bond God gives us as a family. We will feel the love of God that we can share, and that history will live on forever.

If you believe in God, you can look forward to life in heaven.

The following section (to the end of the chapter) comes directly from a wonderful pair of pamphlets titled "Christ Light" NTA & NTB Pre-K-KNT2, "Student Lessons" 72N1211& 72N1221][4]

We should lead lives that are a reflection of the love God has shown us.

It is important for us to praise Jesus, but it is far more important to understand why we do it. Our Lord has done everything to save us, by dying to pay for our sins, and by rising from the dead to assure us of new life in heaven. Jesus is our reason to be happy on earth and our assurance that we will enjoy the happiness of heaven.

Every good and perfect gift is from above (James 1:17); thank God for what He has given us. "Thank you, God, for giving us friends; thank you for cool drinks on a hot day; thank you for so many things to learn."

God truly showers us with blessings, great and small. Let's praise God for His immeasurable love and generosity. Praise the Lord, for He is kind. Every good gift is from Him. Give Him thanks each day in all that you think, say, and do.

"The love of money is a root of all kinds of evil." (Timothy 6:10) The love of money, things, and activities can tempt us to spend little family or worship time together, because we "just have too much work to do."

God warns us not to value our possessions so highly that we lose the treasures we have through faith in our Savior. Learning about the Lord and serving Him should be first in our lives. We should use the many possessions we have to the glory of God and for the benefit of those around us. When we realize God has given us a wealth of gifts, we want to share these gifts with those less fortunate.

Because actions speak louder than words, make time as a family to do something for someone in need.

Trust in the Lord with all your heart. (Proverbs 3:5) Have strong faith in the Savior's power to help us. Pray with confidence. Pray often.

Remember that others' needs may seem insignificant to us, but they can be so important to them.

"Trust in Jesus." Trusting for full salvation, free and true. Trust Jesus to guide you; He alone shall lead. Every day and hour, supplying all our needs.

If we ask anything according to His will, He hears us.

What joy we have in knowing our prayers are heard and answered by God! We can pray to Him with confidence, knowing that He will do what is best, and understanding that God knows better than we do which things are good for us.

Sometimes He will give us what we ask for; other times He may make us wait. At times, He will not give us what we want, just as a loving parent withholds harmful things from a child. God will, in His own time and in his own way, do what is best for our eternal welfare. His love, power, and wisdom are far greater than ours!

How do we receive correction? God shows us in His word the very same message John preached. We sin. Our sinful nature does not like to be corrected. We sometimes get upset with those who remind us of our sins. But, rather than become angry, let us thank God for pastors, teachers, and other Christians who may admonish us. They are concerned about our eternal welfare. When we need to correct someone, let it be obvious that we do it because we care for them.

Where does real love come from?

God. "We love because He first loved us." (John 4:19)

Consider God's will before making decisions. We want our lives to revolve around the love we have for the one who first loved us.

In the Lord's Prayer, Jesus taught us to pray. "Give us today our daily bread." (Matthew 6:10) By praying for daily bread, we are asking God to provide whatever we need to live each day.

Nowhere does he say he will give us a mansion, a yacht, the finest clothing, or gourmet food. "But if we try to count the true needs, He satisfies, plus provides all the extras." He gives. We easily see how loving our God is to us.

The Transfiguration

Jesus looked different. His face was bright like the sun. His clothes were like lightning. They were whiter than anyone could bleach them.

Jesus was transfigured before Peter, James, and John. His appearance changed to show His glory as the Son of God.

Everything about Jesus – who He is, His glory, His power, and His saving love – fills us with wonder and awe. We should speak well of our God. We do not use His name in thoughtless, joking, or disrespectful ways. Instead, we give our God praise.

One day, a man came to Jesus with a question. This man thought he knew the Word of God very well. He asked Jesus, "Teacher, what must I do to have life in heaven?"

Jesus answered the man by asking him a question, "What commands has God written in his word?"

The man answered, "Love the Lord your God. Love your neighbor as yourself." (Matthew 22:39)

"That is right," said Jesus. "Do this and you will live."

Then the man asked, "But who is my neighbor?"

We are all neighbors.

Sometimes we adults notice that children are unloving or downright cruel to other children. Children are sinful, just as we adults are. But children can refer to only a few "serving one another in love" experiences. This is because they have not lived long enough. That's where we come in. We have experienced hurts; we have witnessed the hardships that happen to others. We need to provide opportunities for our children to help needy people so that we can teach what "serving one another in love" is all about. Perhaps we can buy an extra present at Christmas to donate to a needy child. We can stop to speak to a lonely neighbor, or take a hot dish or fruit basket to a family experiencing some kind of difficulty.

It takes effort to serve those in need. But, when we consider the effort that Jesus gave in suffering and dying to earn our salvation, we are more than happy to serve others in love.

God is always ready to bless us spiritually, helping us to grow as we hear and study His Word. He also cares for our physical needs each day. He is with us during times of suffering and trouble, sometimes removing the problems and at other times providing the strength to bear them. We truly do have a loving God, who cares for us as a good shepherd cares for His sheep.

We live in a busy and hectic world; we have responsibilities; we need relaxation. The devil tempts us to think we have no time for anything else.

"Blessed are those who hear the Word of God and obey it." (Luke 11:28) Jesus promises blessings to those who hear His Word. He wants us to look for opportunities to learn more about Him, not just fit Him in when we have time. We should value God's Word when our daily schedule includes time for God. We can plan time for church attendance and daily devotions, just as we plan time for jobs, relaxation, appointments, and errands.

When we read the Bible, listen to a Christian recording, or send a religious greeting card, we are showing we treasure God's Word. We can supply our children with Bible storybooks, recordings of religious songs, and religious items to display in their rooms. These are all ways to focus on the importance of God and His Word in our lives.

May the Lord bless your family as you hear the Word of God, and grow in wisdom and understanding of His Word!

One day, Jesus was speaking with some people who did not believe they needed a Savior to forgive their sins. They thought they did so many good things that God must love them. They also felt that they were better than other people. Jesus wanted to teach these people that they were really sinners who needed a Savior.

All are sinners in need of the Savior. We may be tempted to think that leading a "good" life can earn our salvation. What a mistake to think this way! When we read God's commands, His law, we see that we have not lived the life of perfection that God demands. The perfection that God wants in us, he finds only in his Son.

Jesus Savior, wash away
All that I've done wrong today.
Make me ever more like you:
Good and gentle, kind and true.
(Hymn 593:1,2)

We need to understand about earthly and heavenly treasures.

There was a rich man who had wealth and prestige. He lived in luxury. But he did not care at all about the treasures of God's grace and love. By contrast, Lazarus suffered illness, poverty, and humiliation on earth, but his faith gave him the assurance of forgiveness of sins, and the sure hope of heaven.

There was a complete turnaround when the two men died. The rich man suffered the agonies of hell.

The poor man, who had trusted in the Savior, enjoyed the riches of heaven. This reminds us to never lose sight of the treasures we have through faith in Jesus our Savior.

A materialistic world draws us away from God, to things. Let us, rather, view earthly treasures as gifts from God, and thank Him for them, and value more highly the riches God gives us through faith in Him.

Jesus cries when someone he loves dies. Death brings sadness into our lives as well. But for Christians, death is also a time to thank God for sending us a Savior from sin. Our Lord cares for us even in death. For through it He gives us the gift of life.

Jesus said, "I am the resurrection and the life." (John 11:25) Our Lord is life. He gave us life for us on the cross. He took it back on Easter Sunday. What power! We can be absolutely sure that God, in His love, will pick the perfect time to take us to live with Him in heaven.

We want to show love to Jesus for the wonderful gift of salvation He has won for us. We can offer our praise and thanks to Him. When we make listening to His Word a priority, we are praising Him. When we share His Word with others, we are praising Him. We praise Him as we sing songs, clean the church, and show kindness to others. We do these things gladly out of love for the Savior who first loved us and gave his life for us.

The Lord gives each of us different abilities, and He wants us to use whatever abilities we have to serve Him faithfully. Our God has blessed us with our physical and mental abilities, and our creative talents.

While one person may be an effective speaker, another may be just the listener that others need. While one may be able to lead a large company, another may be able to carry out instructions to the letter, on time. One may have the body build to do heavy lifting, while another may have small, steady hands that can work with tiny electronic devices.

Each of the abilities is different, but all are valuable. All are gifts from a gracious God.

When we remember the best blessing we have from God, we cannot help but show our love and thanks to Him. As we consider the activities in which we participate, we ask ourselves, "Am I using the talents God has given me to serve Him? Is this activity one that God would be pleased with? Am I giving good honor and glory to God by doing this activity?"

May your family make good use of the time and the abilities God has given you, using them to serve Him faithfully in love, and to give Him glory. For whatever you do, do it all for the glory of God. (1 Corinthians 10:31)

The earth is the Lord's and everything in it. (Psalms 24:1)

Expressing the lack of enjoyment in paying taxes is not new. In Jesus' day, the Jews balked at turning their money over to the Roman government. Jesus showed that we have a duty to support the government that God places over us. While we may not agree with all the ways in which the government uses our money, God commands us to obey its laws. By paying the taxes we owe, we follow God's command.

In the Bible, Jesus also reminds us of our duty to the Lord. He reminds us to use our time, our possessions, and our abilities to serve Him. When we remember that the earth is the Lord's and everything in it, we see that God entrusts what is really His to us, while we live on earth. We are happy to use His good gifts to give Him glory, and to thank Him for giving us salvation through Christ Jesus.

When the disciples saw someone walking on the water, they were afraid. They cried out, "It's a ghost!"

But Jesus called to them, saying, "It is I, Jesus. Do not be afraid."

Then Peter said, "Lord, if it is You, tell me to come to You on the water."

"Come," said Jesus.

So Peter got out of the boat and began to walk on water toward Jesus. But when Peter saw how strong the wind and waves were, he became afraid. He began to sink into the water. "Lord, save me!" Peter cried out.

Jesus reached out His hand and caught Peter. Then Jesus said, "Your faith is little, Peter. Why didn't you trust Me?"

Jesus taught his disciples to trust Him in times of trouble. They saw Him walk on water, and quiet the wind and waves.

These miracles convinced the disciples that Jesus was the Son of God. He alone could have such power over nature!

Your child may mention how foolish it was for the disciples to think they were seeing a ghost on the water. But whether children admit it or not, they are often afraid of shadows, noises at night, and imaginary creatures. They need to be reassured of the continual presence of their best friend, Jesus.

Remind your child that Jesus is always nearby, ready to help.

"Call upon Me in the day of trouble; I will deliver you," (Psalms 50:15) is both an invitation and an assurance. Jesus invites us to bring our troubles to Him, and He assures us that He will help. Jesus has the hard part; He alone can either solve our problems or help us through them. He asks us just to do the calling.

Christ Jesus came into the world to save sinners. (1 Timothy 1:15)

Does your family have an answer ready to give when a person asks, "What do you believe about God?"

Questions will come up at work or at social gatherings about what church you attend, and what you believe. Be strong. Be sure.

Rather than saying, "My church teaches," perhaps you could say, "I believe the Bible is God's Word," or "Jesus Christ is the Son of God. He died on the cross to save me from my sins, and rose from the dead. He will give me life in heaven with Him."

Many people in the world need to hear this message come from the lips of Christians – children and adults like us. Our job is to share this message. It is up to God the Holy Spirit to make it blossom into faith.

"Love your neighbor as yourself." (Matthew 22:39)

We know that God has freely forgiven every sin we commit. We ourselves love to hear about the peace we have through the forgiveness of God. We want others to have that same peace. So we share the news of God's forgiveness. We want to carry out God's command to "love your neighbor as yourself" (Matthew 22:39) by forgiving others who sin against us.

Instead of focusing on the wrongs and the hurts that others inflict upon us, we need to remember the pain and suffering that our own sins caused Jesus. Keeping in mind Christ's innocent sufferings and death on our behalf makes it easier for us to forgive others.

Encourage an atmosphere of Christian love and forgiveness in your home by:

1) Praying together for help to forgive others.

2) Apologizing when you sin against someone and forgive others when they sin against you.

God, have mercy on me, a sinner. (Luke 18:13) Our children need to be made aware of the wrongs they do. They need to hear us motivate them to obey God out of love. But they still will fail often, just as we do. They need to know we are there to pick them up and brush them off, just as God lifts and strengthens us with His Word and sends us off again to live for Him.

God's love is constant. Let us help our children see God's unfailing love as we encourage our children to live for Christ.

Give thanks to the Lord, for He is good; His love endures forever. (Psalms 118:1)

You and I often hurry to the Lord in prayer when something devastating comes our way: a sickness, a death in the family, a sudden financial blow, or job loss.

Each day our children and we can thank God by praying:

Dear God,
I thank You for Your love,
love that will never have an end.
Teach me to trust in You each day,
and thank You too,
my dearest friend.
Amen.

God loves us. He teaches us to love ourselves, and to love others.

God forgives us. He teaches us to forgive ourselves, and to forgive others.

God gives us the wisdom to respect and appreciate others, ourselves, and the world we live in.

If we believe in God, we will then begin to experience our purpose in life and find true happiness." [4]

Chapter Three: Living With Healthy Relationships

[I found a lot of my ideas for this chapter from *Codependent No More: How to Stop Controlling Others and Start Caring For Yourself* by Melody Beattie [5] and *Five Love Languages* by, Gary Chapman [6]

Melody Beattie suggests that we don't just *try* to see the goodness and humanity in others; really look for it. Be positive about each relationship. Believe in them as you believe in yourself, giving support when it is appropriate. Some people think they should not be happy, maybe because they don't think they deserve it, or because other people around them are not happy, or if they *are* happy something is bound to go wrong. This is not true. We are all entitled to happiness. Let the good stuff happen! Love your family and learn to let them love you, and always love yourself.

Remember that with any good relationship, there will be times when we need to take care of our own needs first. People will still love you. If you need something, don't cry and whine. Be strong and ask for it straightforwardly, but in a kind and loving way.

Follow your heart in all of your relationships. If it feels right, go for it. If it doesn't, you will know deep inside you. [5]

In any healthy relationship, the truth is always crucial, even when it hurts. In a good relationship, you can be yourself, feel comfortable around the other person, and you will not have to change your lifestyle, friends, or family.

Gary Chapman has several recommendations for us to live by in order to have a healthy relationship, such as spending quality time, listening, talking, and having fun together. Even working together on something you both like to do or have an interest in is considered quality time. Sometimes just being in the same house together can be considered quality time, if you feel content with the other person's presence.

Treat others with kindness, compliments, and stand by them with their wants and needs.

Do things for one another. It could be anything – cooking, cleaning, fixing things, taking out the garbage, keeping up the yard, getting them a glass of water, fixing their hair, and on and on.

Give gifts and learn how to receive them. It is very important to acknowledge someone's birthday. Also, Christmas is a good time to give a gift. It doesn't have to be much; it is the thought that counts.

Depending on the relationship, physical touch is very important. A hug, a touch on the shoulder, holding hands, or if you are married it is very important to make love with your partner. Depending on the couple, how often may vary. You should be able to talk about this because one person may need intimacy more than the other; compromise is a must.

Set goals: things you both want, things you want to do, and things about the relationship you want to work on. [6]

Learn to negotiate. Be clear about what you want and need. Avoid black and white solutions.

Melody Beattie recommends that we set boundaries, defining where you end and another person begins, and if things are not going your way, don't take it personally. It might not have anything to do with you in the first place. Be strong, and don't let people use you. [5]

Never demand in a conflict. Sit down and discuss the problem. Take time out if you have to think about solutions, but don't storm out of the house without saying where you are going and when you will be back. Leaving the other person in the middle of an argument makes it harder on the person who stays because their mind starts wondering, where did they go, who are they with, and are they okay?

If you are married to that person, or if it is your child who lives with you, and they don't come home at night, you will not be able to sleep until they do come back home. If you are dating, your boyfriend or girlfriend shouldn't walk out on you every time you have a disagreement. You need to know where they are going and when they will return. If you are already involved with a walker, face the problem and work it out as a team.

You need at least one best friend of the same sex that you can confide in. This way, when you are having problems with another relationship, you will have a backup, someone who can cheer you up. Maybe you can get their opinion on what is bothering you. Also, someday you can return the favor, when your best friend needs a helping hand. It feels wonderful to be needed.

When you are in a relationship with someone, always make the extra effort to try to better understand the other person, what they are saying and how they feel.

Try to extend your interests at accommodating the other person when appropriate.

Understand what the other's deepest wishes, wants and desires are. Then try your best to provide them.

No one is perfect. Being wise is knowing what to overlook in a relationship.

We all have bad thoughts, but when we speak them aloud or act on those bad thoughts, that's when we start problems in relationships. Taking responsibility and controlling our emotions is a must.

Some words are better left unsaid when used in a negative manner or during an argument, like "always" and "never" or "forever." Instead, use words like "sometimes" – it sounds less permanent.

Unless people ask for your advice, don't pry into their business. Even if you think they need your advice, wait until they want to discuss it.

Avoid trying to convince the other of something they don't want to be convinced of.

Expecting the other to know what you are thinking or feeling is not going to work; people cannot read your mind. You have to tell them, so they know. At first it may be difficult, but as time goes by it will get easier to talk about what is on your mind or what you are feeling. Also, don't try to tell the other person what he or she is thinking or feeling. Ask them, if you think something is bothering them. Maybe you could help in some way.

Criticizing can be beneficial if it is done constructively and respectfully. If you must criticize, criticize a specific part of his or her behavior. Don't criticize the person. An example would be: "It bothers me when you don't call if you're going to be late" instead of saying "You're always late."

Avoid grave digging – throwing up the past to open up old wounds. Also, there is no need to point fingers at who is right or wrong, and don't keep score whose turn it is to apologize or give in. Send the message "I feel…" rather than "you make me feel…"

Gary Chapman has eight simple guidelines for a happy marriage.

What keeps some people happily married?

1) Trust between the partners.

2) Enjoyment of each other.

3) An assumption of permanence in the relationship.

4) An ability to change, and to tolerate change.

5) A willingness to live with the things one cannot change.

6) A shared history that is cherished.

7) A balance of power.

8) A balance of depending on one another. [6]

Unfortunately, because it is human nature, there will be times when we will have to deal with lying.

Why do people lie? We lie because we are scared, ashamed, or to cover up the truth. Sometimes we lie to get out of a frightening situation, or to save someone else's feelings. Some people lie because they are confused or just plain mean. You may lie because you are embarrassed about a silly mistake you have made and want to let it go. We have all done it. We have all lied.

For the most part, most people try to live their lives in an honest manner so that they can avoid lying. Once you start lying you can quickly get caught in the lying web, and cannot find our way out. Your whole life can be based on so many lies that you start getting confused and start believing the lies are true. Then you have problems, because if you cannot be true to yourself, you will not be content or happy. A sense of shame will be all around you. Now there are only two ways out. Go back and say you're sorry and tell the truth, or move away and start anew.

Signs to look for if you think someone is lying to you: if they turn away, if they cannot look you in the eye when they answer you, if they give you an indirect answer, if they don't answer at all, or if there is a change in their voice.

Please remember that we all lie. If you confront a person about lying, they will most likely feel shame. Sit down with them and, in a kind and loving way, remind them that sometimes you lie, too. This will break the ice, and maybe he or she will open up and be truthful. If they will not open up with the truth, try to let it go if it is a minor issue. However, if you notice that the lying is constant, you may both need to seek help to save the relationship.

As children, we cannot pick and choose our families. We try to accept our families the way they are. But please remember that we have a choice of whom we want in our lives as adults. We are whom we live with and spend time with. If we are with good, loving people, we will be good and loving also.

Do not ever underestimate how important this is, especially if we have children or grandchildren, because it will affect them all through their lives. This is when we have to look for our inner child. Be strong and tell yourself, "I don't need these bad people in my life" and "I can find better people to share my life with." This includes family members, especially if someone in your family is sexually, physically, or mentally abusing you, if they are cheating on you, if they don't spend quality time with you, or if they steal from you and won't seek help. Move on to a better life, because you will never have true happiness if you have unhealthy relationships in your life.

Look at your inner child and tell yourself, "I am not taking care of my own health and needs by letting these people treat me and my children so disrespectfully."

Then you will have true happiness.

Chapter Four: Healthy Dating

Finding the love of your life is a challenge because dating is so hard these days. I know, because I was in a long-term relationship, and when it ended I thought to myself, how will I ever meet someone again?

My psychotherapist suggested to me to get over my grief and find my inner child before I start dating again. I waited seven months and I can tell you, she was right. I was not ready, and wished I had waited longer.

This is a good time to find your inner child. For me, this was the first time I have ever lived alone. I felt lonely and yet content. It was nice to just eat when I wanted, sleep when I wanted, and do what I wanted whenever I wanted. I spent a lot of time with my family and friends. I think the intimacy was what I longed for. Also, romantic love is different than the love of a child, grandchild, mother, father, brother, sister or friend. Maybe that is why so many people get married even though divorce rates are so high.

I was happy and content without a man. I had a good job and I knew that I could make it on my own. But all my children were grown, all my friends and family had families of their own. I dated because I wanted to share my love, intimacy, and life with someone.

But there wasn't anyone I knew who was single. My friend had a neighbor that she introduced me to, but when I dated him, I felt like he was mentally abusing me. It only lasted about four or five months. I also dated a man who I had met casually. But that did not last either because I felt that he was abusing alcohol.

I tend to be more of a homebody and did not want to go to the bars just to meet someone, so I started dating online. I met some strange men! Some men were afraid of a relationship. Some only wanted sex and some men just scared me. I dated casually for three and a half years before I found the love of my life. Yes, I said it, I met him online!

His name is Kevin. I liked his profile and picture, he was nice-looking and we emailed back and forth for about two weeks. Then we talked on the phone for about a week. I made sure that I used a number that he could not trace back to where I lived. At this time we had only given each other our first names.

Now for the hard part of dating: Meeting a stranger for the first time! Our first date was at a local restaurant for a fish dinner. He wasn't the type of man I would normally have dated. In the past I typically dated men who were very quiet and shy. Kevin was more outgoing. It wasn't love at first sight, however. But he looked exactly like his picture. Kevin is tall and very nice-looking. The whole evening just flowed. He was interesting and was genuinely interested in me. We had a lot of eye contact. I felt like I could trust him.

He asked me if I wanted to see a movie and I said yes. I should have followed him there but I felt so confident that I got into his car and went to see a movie with him. At one point he took a wrong turn and I thought, "Oh my God! What have I gotten myself into?" It was okay, but through my experience I would not advise such trust in anyone on the first date. So at this point I got his whole name and looked him up online to make sure that he had no criminal record.

Good to go! Now we could start dating. He would pick me up at my house and we would go and do fun things together. On one of our dates we went to his house for dinner, so I took this opportunity to prove to myself that he was not married or living with someone else by looking into his closet. To my relief there were only his clothes. You can find out if someone is divorced online, but it does not guarantee that they have not remarried. But because of one of my past experiences I was direct and asked him straight out if he was married our seeing anyone.

One of the things that I knew I didn't want to do was get involved with someone who abused drugs or alcohol. A person can easily hide something like that for a while if you tell them that you will not tolerate it. So in order to make sure that Kevin did not abuse drugs or alcohol, I kept my eyes open for signs that might indicate that Kevin had a drug or alcohol problem. I didn't ask him this directly, however, because he could have easily kept his abuse hidden from me.

A lot of times in a relationship, this is when denial will start. Melody Beattie suggests denial is when you bury the truth about something deep inside of you, in fear of losing love, trust, relationships, or your dreams. It would hurt too much. You need to become safe and strong enough to cope with reality. Eventually denial will surface, and you will see the truth when you are ready. [5]

Knowing this, I made sure that we had time away from each other. It is easier to see the truth, the good and bad about each other, when you are on the outside looking in. If the other person seems to be smothering you, there could be a reason why. Keep an eye on your inner child. Remember you can live without this person.

In a past relationship I was with a person who was evasive. I knew from past experience that I didn't want to get involved again with an evasive person.

Evasive people can be dishonest. They may not be straightforward with you. You don't want to be with someone who is evasive because they will surprise you someday and you will be in for a shock.

If you ask a question like, "Did you have sex with her?" They may reply by saying, "I didn't even kiss her" instead of giving you a straight yes or no answer. Evasive people also won't take your direct answer seriously. They may assume that you are also being indirect.

So far, so good. Kevin is so direct, just like me, he is a breath of fresh air. No drug or alcohol abuse to my knowledge.

So now we are ready to meet our family and friends. All of my family really liked him, especially my grandchildren, who seem to have fun with him. I liked all of his family and friends. He treated me the same when we were with them as when we were alone. It made me feel that I was good enough.

Based on my past experiences with men who seemed to hate their mothers, deep inside I think they also hated me. This is one of the reasons why I fell in love with Kevin: he is the first man that I have ever been with that truly loves me. I know that he loved his mother just by the way he talks about her, thinks about her and took care of her before she died. Just the way that he touched me was different than any way that I had ever been touched before.

My mother is now 88 years old. Kevin and I talked about my mother possibly moving in with me because of her health. I was worried about what Kevin would think about my mother possibly moving in with me and he told me that he would have thought less of me if I had not helped my mother when she needed me most.

I feel like he is the very first man I have ever been with that really loved his mother.

I feel like he is my best friend. We have so many things in common. We are both spiritual and love the holidays with family and friends. We have been through so many of the same family experiences it is almost scary. We both love children! We also share a passion for the same activities. In short, we love to spend time together; I never want him to go home.

After dating for a while you may both be ready for a serious commitment to each other. You are just going to know! There won't any doubts or second thoughts in your mind. It will just feel right!

This is what happened to me. It just felt right! It must have also felt right for Kevin because after several months of dating, he asked me to marry him. I said yes – because it just felt right!

One of the things I love about him is that I feel like I can trust him. Early on in our relationship, Kevin gave me a promise ring. That was a big step in our relationship because he was telling me that he would be faithful to me and that I could trust him. Because if you don't have trust you don't have anything!

In any marriage there will be temptations.

You may find yourself attracted to another person, and you'll need to be strong enough to tell yourself the lust is not worth ending your relationship.

Some of the main reasons why I think Kevin and I have such a great relationship is because we can talk to each other about anything and because we make it a point to have fun. For us, even planning our wedding has been a great source of fun and enjoyment.

If a relationship is going to work, both partners are equals. This is how Kevin and I have treated each other from day one. I am no better than him and he is no better than me. Because we are equals, all decisions are and always will be joint decisions.

After you are married and you start living together there will naturally be changes and adjustment that will be required. It will be different from living alone. Don't try to change the other person. You will be living as one, but you will still be your own selves, meaning there will be things that you won't agree on or thing you may not even like about each other. Accept one another for who they are.

Being a team will keep you together. One doesn't feel like they need to control the other person. This is how you can stay best friends.

In your life as one, there will be times when you will need to depend on one another. If you are there for each other, the bond will be stronger in time.

Why did we decide to get married instead of just living together? Because in our eyes it is the respectable thing to do for two people who want to spend the rest of their lives together. The statistics show that more couples cheat on one another when they just live together. It makes sense, because when you are dating, you are looking at the future. When you get married it is a commitment, that if one cheats they will feel shamed, but if you just live together it is like saying, "I want my cake and eat it too." The other bad thing about just living together is that if someone wants to break up, it is harder to distribute your belongings fairly.

After the wedding, the most important thing to remember is to treat your husband or wife the way you want to be treated.

Someday, maybe years later, your lives may start to drift apart. This is the main reason why couples break up. If you really love one another, seek help and work it out. This is because true love is so hard to find, and once it is gone you may never find true love again.

Sometimes it seems easier to walk away than to try to solve your problems. You both need to be strong and help one another as a family should do.

In a good loving marriage, you can have true love and happiness. All it takes is wisdom, forgiveness, and love.

If your heart is in it, you will become one.

Chapter Five: Understanding and Dealing with Depression

One thing that can affect our happiness is depression. Anyone can get it, and at any time. It just creeps up on you. You may have depression and not even know it. Understanding depression is the first step you need to take to keep it out of your life.

I did a lot of research concerning depression and I found that Dr. Charles E. Martin summed it up best in the following section from "Depression vs. Sadness / The Types of Depression or Mood Disorders"

http://www.clinicalpsychologist.com/

depression.html"

"Depression vs. Sadness: Understanding the Difference

When are feelings of sadness, gloom, or "feeling down" normal, and when are they a more serious problem? It is normal to feel sad at times. Normal sadness usually does not affect all areas of a person's life and generally goes away in a few hours or days. Sometimes doing something pleasurable, like a shopping trip with friends, will cause sadness to lighten.

Clinical depression differs from normal sadness or "the blues" in both the severity of symptoms and in duration. Clinical depression lasts for much longer periods of time and has more symptoms. The rule of thumb is that if sadness lasts longer than two weeks, it is probably clinical depression. This type of depression often interferes with everyday functioning. Clinical depression is a serious disorder that needs to be evaluated by a professional and usually requires some form of treatment.

Types of depression or mood disorders

Situational Depression occurs when the depression is a reaction to some event or circumstance in a person's life. This form of depression is usually associated with some loss or perceived loss, such as loss of job, divorce, death, breakup of a relationship, or children leaving home.

Biological Depression: [Depression of this type seems to occur completely "out of the blue." It] is caused by a chemical imbalance in the neurochemistry of the brain and is not associated with events occurring in a person's life.

Dysthymic Disorder is a long-term or chronic problem. It may be quite wide-ranging in the way it affects a person's life. Sometimes it is a low-grade form of depression. It often appears like a "depressed personality." Often people with this disorder report feeling depressed most of their life, starting in childhood or teenage years. The symptoms may not interfere with daily functioning, but the person just does not feel well.

Cyclothymic Disorder: A mood disorder characterized by more than normal moodiness and changes of affect. Often appears as an extremely moody person, with mood shifts from serious depression to overly energetic and almost manic behavior. However, the mood shifts are not enough to cause the individual to be unable to function.

Bipolar Disorder: This used to be called manic-depressive disorder. It is caused by a chemical imbalance in the brain and usually is characterized by periods of extremely low depression and feeling "at the bottom," which cycles into periods of boundless energy, grandiose planning, elated moods, and being "on top of the world." The mood shifts are so extreme as to cause the person to be unable to function, cope, or make good judgment or decisions. The moods can cycle from one phase to another quite rapidly or very slowly, lasting for weeks or months. Bipolar disorder almost always requires medication as part of treatment.

Seasonal Affective Disorder (SAD): This is actually a subtype of depression rather than a separate form of depression. It results from changes in the body chemistry due to reduced periods of sunlight, and therefore more common during winter months and in northern areas. Most people with SAD feel better when the spring/summer seasons arrive and the days are longer.

Postpartum Depression: This type of depression may occur after the birth of a child and is often called the "baby blues."

Masked Depression: This is actually a description of a process rather than a diagnostic category. Masked depressions do not appear as depression on the surface, but has behaviors present that cover or "mask" an underlying depression. That is, the individual may have an underlying form of depression which has not been recognized or formally diagnosed. The person uses behaviors which are attempts to make them feel better, such drinking, drug use, sexual acting out, risk-taking behaviors, and other forms of self-destructive behavior. Once diagnosed, treatment of the underlying problem often results in the reduction of the "self-treatment" behaviors." [7]

Understanding symptoms of depression
1. Loss of interest/pleasure in ordinary activities.
2. Changes in appetite and sleep.
3. Fatigue or loss of energy.
4. Feelings of worthlessness or guilt.
5. Trouble thinking, concentrating, or making decisions.
6. Thoughts of death or suicide.

Life is so complex. Now that we understand the type of depression and symptoms of depression, we need to understand how we can keep depression out of our lives.

Here comes your inner child again. Because keeping depression out of your life starts with you – how you feel about yourself and how you see the world around you. Build a satisfying and meaningful life is one of the most important things we can do. Keep in mind, however, that some types of depression do require professional help.

"Take a moment to appreciate what is great about your life. It is instant therapy.

"Gratitude is like a flashlight, shining on what is good. When you turn it on, you feel happier, no matter what else is going on. Science is now confirming the power of a good attitude. Studies show that being grateful increases happiness by 25 percent, and boosts the amount of time that people spend exercising.

"This is wonderful because people who exercise are happier than people who don't" [3]

The best exercises are ones you enjoy. Perhaps that includes swimming, biking, horseback riding, sledding, bowling, snow-shoeing, skiing, and so on. If it is fun, you will be able to stay in shape and feel better about yourself. Not just because of the way you look, but also because of the way you feel inside.

"Being positive even seems to create greater equality in dividing up chores between partners.

The great thing about the gratitude flashlight: it works no matter who you are – young or old, heavy or thin, rich or poor, sick or well. All you need to do is turn it on." [3]

Ways to show gratitude

Here comes God again. Remember, when God reminds us to give thanks for our daily bread, this is gratitude. Before we eat, it is a good habit to thank God for the food we are about to eat.

Think of why you love your spouse, children, and friends every day.

Don't compare your life with others, keeping up with the neighbors. Make your life comfortable for you. Think about what you need in your life to make you happy, not others.

Look at your body in the mirror every morning and see one thing you like about it. Now see one thing you don't like about it and make it your goal to work on that. It will give you something to look forward to.

Look for hidden blessings in your life. How have you grown?

When you go to bed at night, ask God for one thing you would like, and thank God for one thing in your life.

Look at everyday things in your life positively. Don't be unhappy that you have to clean the house; be happy you have a house to clean. Don't be unhappy you have to go to work, be happy you have a job at all, and so on and so on. If you really look, you can find good in almost everything.

Look back at your life so far. You probably could have had it a lot better than what you did, but if you really think about it, things could have been a lot worse.

Gratitude is a way to keep depression away. Remember, if you put on a sad face, you will be sad. If you put on a happy face, you will be happy.

Now that we have a good attitude, we can move on to other things in our life to keep depression away unless it is determined that professional help is required.

Write down two activities to do that day, and do them. Keeping busy is very good to stimulate the brain. Find a state park and go for a walk. Appreciate the scenery and wildlife, because when it comes to nature, life is beautiful.

Do things you enjoy; go see a movie, find a new or old hobby and work on that, or just hang out with family and friends. Talk about your day.

Get outside in the sun between 10:00 a.m. and 3:00 p.m. Bright light has been shown to have an antidepressant effect on the body. Light is especially good if you suffer from seasonal affective disorder.

Before you get out of bed in the morning, take some time to think about what tasks you would like to accomplish, and in what order, from the most important to the least important. Be realistic about what you will accomplish throughout that day. Taking on too many responsibilities will only set you up for failure, which brings on depressive feelings.

Look back at situational depression. It could be a job loss, divorce, death, breakup of a relationship, or children leaving home. These situations could happen any time in your life. They are pretty obvious, and most people get over this depression after they have allowed themselves to go through the emotions of their loss, because as time goes by the heartache tends to fade. When you think about these particular situations, tell yourself, "I can't change or fix it." The one thing you can change and fix is your personal well-being. Letting go and accepting what has happened allows you to take care of yourself. If you feel healthiest, you can be there for all the people you love, including yourself.

Now look back at masked depression. These are forms of depression that do not appear as depression on the surface, but have behaviors that serve to threat, cover, or "mask" an underlying depression. People cause this depression, with things that are so damaging you cannot face them directly. Someone may have sexually abused you, physically abused you, or mentally abused you. Not knowing how to handle this pain that a person has inflicted on you will cause you to fall into a masked depression. In some way, it will haunt you for the rest of your life, and it will actually change your personality. This is where you will need God in your life. God says, "Forgive those who trespass against us." (Matthew 6:12) Until we can understand why people do these things to others, and until we can forgive them, we will never find true happiness. But if you learn to forgive the person who did this traumatic thing to you, have the wisdom to stop the abuse, and find love for yourself (your inner child) once again, you will find true happiness.

Chapter Six: Understanding and Dealing with Drugs and Alcohol

"Alcohol disrupts your REM sleeping patterns. You won't dream because your body is being deprived of your deepest sleep.

"You may sleep seven to eight hours a night, but it is not a good, sound sleep. This is why it is so important to only have one drink a day for women, and two drinks a day for men. Because if you are an alcoholic, you may find yourself drinking more to fall asleep, and if this pattern does not stop, your overall health will decrease in time. Irreversible brain damage may occur.

Happiness and awareness of your soul and inner child will be taken away from you, because alcohol consumption actually tends to lessen the occurrence of dreaming and nightmares. It also numbs the pain of emotions." [2]

The key to letting go of problems in your life is to let the emotions out and simply deal with what is bothering you. If you cover up your emotions with drugs and alcohol, you will not get over the pain someone has inflicted on you. This is very important so you can let it go and move on with your life.

Do not let drugs and alcohol abuse in your life. The addictions that come with it can destroy everyone involved.

Five Possible Addictions

1) Sex – cannot stay with one partner.
2) Physical – hitting.
3) Mental – verbal abuse.
4) Gambling – gambling money you don't have.
5) Dysfunctional – abnormal or impaired functioning. Can't function without a drink under stressful situations. May not be able to keep a job if the problems get too bad.

Possible Signs of an Alcoholic

1. You drink to get drunk.
2. You drink when it doesn't taste good.
3. You change when you drink.

1) You catch yourself thinking, or saying to someone, "You make me drink."
2) Under stressful situations, you find yourself needing a drink.

If you think you might have a problem with drugs or alcohol, take the challenge. Don't do any drugs or alcohol for six months, after first seeking the advice of a physician. Some addicts may need to go to a hospital for supervised detoxification, because suddenly withdrawing from drugs or alcohol can be harmful and/or fatal.

It might be hard to abstain from alcohol or drugs, depending on your lifestyle. If you socialize with people who do drugs or drink alcohol, you may have to let these people know you are taking the challenge. Be honest and if they keep pressuring you to drink or do drugs with them, you will have to be strong enough to realize these people are not good for you.

This is when you need to look back at your inner child. Tell yourself you do not want to live like this anymore. Say, "I don't need these people in my life. I can live without these people. I can find better people to be with; people that will help me take the challenge and will be better for me."

After six months, if you were able to stay away from drugs and alcohol, you should be fine. Drugs should never be taken again. Alcoholics should not drink again. Only those who are considered social drinkers and are NOT alcoholics can once again consume alcohol, in moderation. Rule of thumb: one drink a day for women equals one glass of wine, one shot if you have a mixed drink, or one 12-ounce beer. For men, two glasses of wine, two shots if you have a mixed drink, or two 12-ounce beers. This does not mean you can bank your drinks, meaning if you don't drink all week you can drink more on the weekends.

Remember, no one is pouring alcohol down your throat, and no one is making you take drugs. It is no one's responsibility but your own.

If you realize that you are an alcoholic or are addicted to drugs, my heart goes out to you. No one should ever look down on you because it can happen to anyone. But, please remember, the first step to getting help is to accept the fact that you are sick.

Accept the fact that your addiction may be caused by depression, and know that if you don't get help for your sickness, you shall never find true happiness. This is when you will need to be very strong to face things that have happened to you in the past. Be wise, like an old owl, to help you understand why these things happened to you in the first place. Learn to forgive the people who have put you through so much torment that you turned to alcohol or drugs to cope with your life. Lastly, learn to forgive yourself for the way you are. Find your inner child again (love for yourself).

Then you will find true happiness again.

Living on the other side of alcohol and drugs.

You could be an enabler or be codependent. An enabler is someone who makes it easier for an alcoholic to get alcohol, who can't be strong enough to help the alcoholic resist.

Being codependent is the role that the enabler plays to cope with the alcoholic. Codependency is anytime you put someone else before yourself. One very important thing you need to understand is if an alcoholic has an enabler, he or she has a lesser chance of getting help. When alcoholics have no one to blame but themselves, they will have a better chance at getting help. This is called hitting rock bottom. If you are living with an alcoholic and he or she decides they won't seek help, and you decide to leave them, this is called tough love. The addict has no control over his or her addiction, and for this reason they should seek professional help.

But *you* have control over your decision of whether to stay in an alcoholic or drug-addicted relationship or not. This is when you need to find your inner child. This will help you understand that you only need yourself. This is when you will have to be wise as an old owl, to help you understand what is involved with alcoholic relationships. Lastly, after you have moved beyond this failed relationship, you need to forgive this person who has taken away your dreams.

All of this applies to drug users as well.

I kept this chapter for last because many people, at some point in their lives, have felt the effect of drugs and alcohol in some way, and when it happens you can never find true happiness.

It is very painful to see someone you love have an addiction, and to feel powerless to help.

Now we are ready to understand what your life could be like while living with an alcoholic or drug user.

They may cut you down; it is because they need to feel superior over you. Tell them to stop it, or tune it out.

Anger, rage, complaining, and whining are all clues to boundaries. We need to set boundaries when we are feeling threatened, suffocated, or victimized.

They may have a fragile personality. They feel easily invalidated and react with rage at the smallest infraction. So if a person crosses a boundary into their territory, it's not like a tap on the shoulder, it's like a punch in the back.

Feuding behavior is common. If a family member doesn't side with them, they feel betrayed. Trying to make peace with them often doesn't work, because it makes them feel justified. If their behavior escalates you have to be firm and tell them that it's over the line.

As written in *Beyond Betrayal: Taking Charge of Your Life After Boyhood Sexual Abuse* by Richard Gartner [8]:

"If you are with a sex-addicted person, he or she will have multiple partners. They don't necessarily like the sex – they like being able to say "I can get him or her." [8]

With regard to gambling money they don't have, if you stay with someone like this, you will have financial problems.

With physical abuse, they will hit you or someone you love, or both.

With mental abuse, they will verbally abuse you or someone you love, or both.

With regard to being dysfunctional, they may not be able to keep a job or function under normal situations.

All domestic abuse is caused by a need for control and power.

Control and power

Following is some helpful information from *The Power and Control Wheel, Equality Wheels*, Domestic Abuse Intervention Project [9] on how to tell if your living with an abuser:

"Using intimidation – using looks, actions, and gestures to make another person fearful; smashing things, abusing pets, or displaying weapons.

"Using emotional abuse – putting someone down by calling names, telling someone they are crazy, playing mind games, and using humiliation and guilt to control another person.

"Using isolation – controlling every aspect of what another person does, who they see and talk to, and where they go; also limiting partner's outside involvement, and using jealousy to justify this action.

"Minimizing, denying and blaming – making light of the abuse or not taking the victim's concerns about it seriously; denying the abuse happened; shifting responsibility for abusive behavior; saying the victim asked for or caused it.

"Using children – making the partner feel guilty about children; using the children to relay messages; asking children about the partner's activities; threatening to take children away; trying to make the children hate the partner by saying bad things about them.

"Using special privilege – treating the partner as insignificant; making all the decisions; always being right; infringing on your partner's right to make decisions for themselves; forcing your partner to accept your way of thinking.

"Using economic abuse – preventing the partner from getting or keeping a job; making your partner ask for money or live on an allowance; making the partner hand over their paycheck; not sharing information about family income.

"Using coercion and threats – making and carrying out threats to do something to hurt another person; threatening to hurt someone; to commit suicide; to report alleged misconduct to welfare; pressuring the victim to drop charges and/or do illegal things.

"These are all signs to watch out for. These are ways that the abuser tries to maintain power and control in their relationships. All abuse is intentional, used to gain power and control over another person. Violence is never an isolated behavior. Please get help. You don't have to live that way." [9]

Below is an excerpt from *The Battered Woman* by Lenore E. Walker [10]:

"The Cycle of Violence

While the length and circumstances of each case may vary, the pattern formed in abusive relationships is predictable and usually becomes more severe over time.

Phase One: The tension-building stage can last for years. Coping mechanisms used by victims are:

1) <u>Denial</u> of the abuse.

2) <u>Rationalization</u> – victims excuse the abuse as situational.

3) Victims become more passive, and perpetrators become more aggressive.

4) Victims withdraw, staying out of the perpetrator's way or attending to their whims.

5) Perpetrators become more possessive jealous, and oppressive out of fear of losing the victim.

Phase Two: A violent incident occurs. The incident may be triggered by an external event, such as loss of a job, pregnancy, financial pressure, or even sometimes by the victim. The victim cannot take the anxiety any longer and creates the explosion. At least then the victim has control over when and why, rather than being totally at the mercy of the perpetrator. Difficult to predict. Only perpetrators can end Phase Two. Dissociation by victim – the victim doesn't resist, and feels painless.

The victim doesn't usually seek help during this period.

The violent incident is followed by reactions of shock, denial, and disbelief by both partners.

Victim remains isolated for the first 24-48 hours afterwards.

Abuse occurs then the perpetrator feels a loss of control.

Phase Three: Kindness and loving behavior. Shorter than Phase One, but longer than Phase Two. It follows immediately after Phase Two. When the perpetrator is ready to accept new ideas, suggestions, etc., only then can his efforts win the victim back. They will work on the victim's guilt.

The victim wants to help the perpetrator.

The perpetrator may threaten suicide.

The victim sees the perpetrator's insecurities.

Bonding occurs – both are dependent on each other.

This is the most difficult time for the victim to make decisions because they don't want to lose their dreams of the relationship. What should you do if you are caught up in this vicious cycle? Seek help right away. The victims and children of such a cycle will live in constant fear of when it will happen again, and it will. Violence is a family problem. Children who witness such acts will come to accept this behavior as normal." [10] Or they may become perpetrators themselves unless they get help and counseling.

If all else fails, try counseling or the vicious cycle will most likely happen again. Move on with your life.

Remember, you will never find true happiness if you are a victim.

Conclusion: Sharing a Little of Myself

I would like to close this book by telling you a little about myself.

I am not a teacher, doctor, or psychotherapist. I am a dysfunctional child in midlife. I have had many chapters in my life, as this book has. There have been times in my life that I wasn't truly happy.

When I was about 10 years old, a family member started sexually abusing me. When I was 12 years old, I got my period, and suddenly I woke up. "My God, what is going on here is not right." Suddenly I got very angry and started to hate myself for being so stupid. I felt shame so bad I fell into a masked depression. I was in this depression for about four years of my life. I did drugs, I drank alcohol, I had sexual encounters, and I ended up having a baby boy when I was 16 years old. Because of this I had lost my true happiness – all this time in my life.

Do you believe in love at first sight? Trust me when I say it does happen. As soon as I saw my baby, I was in love. This is what brought true happiness back into my life. Now I had a purpose in life, to take care of my baby. To this day, I love him with all my heart. I was no longer depressed. My baby saved me. Even though having a baby out of wedlock is not accepted, it was like God knew what I needed to start getting better.

After I had my baby, I got an infection in my stitches. I was in so much pain I told my dad that I couldn't go to church that day. Being the religious zealot that he was, he judged me and told me I didn't have to go to church anymore, because I was going to hell. I was thinking to myself, he doesn't even know what happened to me, why I am this way. I thought to myself, "But Dad, I love going to church. How can you take that away from me?"

To this day, as I am sitting here writing these words, it is the most painful thing I have ever encountered and the oldest wound that will probably never heal. My face feels warm as the tears develop into my eyes. But my mom kept me together. She told me,

"Dad doesn't realize how much pain you are in from the infection, and you truly are not going to hell."

The reason I am sharing this with you is because I don't want you to finish this book thinking, "Yeah, she probably had a great life – which is why she has found true happiness." But you see it was my attitude. I could have turned against God and my dad, but I didn't. I was wise enough to see that my dad had a sickness about religion, and I couldn't let him take God away from me because I found pleasure in God. I still loved God, but my dad stopped taking me to church. This was very painful for me because the love of God was the only bond I had with my dad. Even though my dad never told me that he loved me, not even on his deathbed, I know he loved me because he let me keep my baby.

Now I had a wonderful boyfriend (I will call him Tony) and a baby. We were like a little family. We were best friends and did everything together. Years later he called me up and he told me he was leaving me for someone else. I was heartbroken. I started feeling suicidal. I felt like a part of me had died, crying the tears of pain for weeks.

Then one day he called me and told me his girlfriend had left him for another, and "Can I come back?" I said, "I don't want you back!" and that was then end of it. I couldn't stand the thought of being with him after he was with her. My heart wasn't in it.

Now, how would you have felt about this person? My attitude was positive. I thought to myself, he is a very respectful man to leave me first, instead of cheating on me. I don't think he cheated on me, but if he did at least he didn't try to keep both of us. I know he was sorry for what he did to our relationship, but we were both young, and to this day I love him for respecting me and giving me years of his life. That truly helped me see the good in men.

After that, I was on my own with my son, and I still was truly happy. The only thing missing in my life was the love of a man.

Then I met my husband (I will call him Rick) through a friend. I didn't love him, but he wanted to get married and have a baby. Because I wanted a man in my life to fill the emptiness, because I wanted to have another baby, and because it was the appropriate thing to do, I married him. He treated me like a queen, and was very good to my son.

But after we had our baby girl together, Rick changed like Dr. Jekyll to Mr. Hyde. I found myself in a drug and alcohol relationship. He had two addictions, and he was physically and mentally abusive. Because of this my son wanted to live with my parents. It was harder for him because he was brought into the relationship when I married Rick, whereas my daughter was born into the relationship so it wasn't as hard on her. It was the only life she knew.

One thing you have to know is if you are in an abusive relationship it affects the whole family so my son moved in with his grandparents. I lost my true happiness for nine years. I tried counseling with him, but it didn't help. I ended up in the hospital with a nervous breakdown. When the divorce was final, it was the happiest day of my life. I wasn't a victim anymore.

I could have hated him, and men altogether, but I didn't. I had a good attitude about the situation and was grateful to look back at my own past and see how fortunate I was that I didn't get addicted to drugs and alcohol when I was depressed. I also had a daily reminder of my beautiful daughter we had together. He had loved me. He let me keep the house we had purchased together. I was content and found true happiness once again.

One year later, I met a man at work (I will call him Jason). We were together for many years. At the time, he was the love of my life. I will never regret being with him. He made me who I am today. He was good to me and to my family. He spent quality time with me. He never hit me or mentally abused me in any way, as far as I could see at the time. He bought me gifts, and we traveled together. I thought I'd never have the opportunity to do that again. He did love me. True happiness was with me for the longest period of my life. This is when I started having a relationship with my son again.

But something didn't feel right about us. I never wanted to marry him. I wasn't sure what was wrong, because I lost myself to denial in this relationship. On the surface, it was perfect. Did you ever hear the saying, if it seems too good to be true, it probably is? Somewhere deep inside of me, I was second-guessing myself. Instead of being strong and trusting my instincts about Jason, I kept thinking it was only in my head, that having been sexually abused was making me think he was having sex behind my back. I was a victim of an alcohol and sex-addicted man, and I didn't even realize it until after he had left me.

Now I'm on the outside looking in. I wasn't in denial anymore. Things were clearing in my head. Seven months into that relationship, Jason had a party at his apartment. He was very drunk and started flirting with another woman, right in front of his mom and dad, and me. He was also making faces at me, as though I was fat. I was so disgusted that I left the party.

Now, if I had had the wisdom of knowing about alcoholism and the addictions that went with it, I probably would have been smart enough to end the relationship. The next day he said, "I'm sorry. I didn't know what I was doing. I was drunk." I should have said, "Then you need to get help." But instead, I took him back, because I was already in love with him. I started controlling him, making sure we stayed away from other women and heavy drinking, because every time we did party, he would hang on the prettiest girl there. Sometimes it was myself.

The whole time I was with him, I would have nightmares about men raping me. Things got worse after I sold my house and we bought a house together. I started feeling sick. One day he came home late and asked me what I wanted for dinner. I said, "It doesn't matter to me, because I don't feel good, and nothing tastes good to me."

I was so sick to my stomach that my bones ached. It was like I couldn't stretch enough. I was bleeding in the rectum. At times I couldn't even work.

I remember telling people that I felt sick. I also told my boss at work, "I don't know how much longer I can do my job."

Also, all the time we lived in that house together, I was having nightmares. Men kept chasing me. I would try to call for help, but I couldn't get the numbers right. I would freeze up. Sometimes I would try to run away, but my feet wouldn't move. Right before Jason left me, I had a nightmare that a man killed me. I would wake up in a cold sweat every time. In the nightmare where the man killed me, as I was dying, I kept saying, "Tell my children I love them," over and over again.

After he left me, all my nightmares stopped immediately, and I have never had nightmares like that to this day. Also, shortly after he left, I started feeling better physically. I even stopped bleeding in the rectum.

It was the oddest breakup I have ever had. The morning after he left, he came and took every pill in the house – a whole drawer full of herb pills. The odd thing about it was he didn't take anything else with him, not even his clothes. I think he was aware of my denial surfacing and felt his control over me was fading. My psychotherapist also pointed out the fact that after we bought the house together he could have been feeling guilty and ashamed about what he was doing behind my back. Maybe the commitment to the house broke us up.

I realize how important it is to trust your instincts and pay attention to your nightmares. It shocks me to this day that I could be with someone so dangerous for so many years. I could have gotten AIDS or another sexually transmitted disease. I also realize how close I was to dying. My heart ached so bad that I thought I was going to die, and yet I was happy. Why do you think that just after losing the love of my life at that time– my best friend – and not quite knowing what was happening to our relationship, that I was still happy, almost feeling free as a bird flying in the sky?

It was my attitude about my whole life and myself. I actually love myself. I know I'm not perfect, but I treated him the way I wanted to be treated. I was stronger than I had ever been before. I was living in my dream home. I had felt the love of a man for many years; I had two beautiful children who loved me; I had a best friend of the same sex whom I could confide in. I was free, but very confused and shocked.

Listed below are several questions that the Madison Women's Clinic's *Once Upon a Thigh blog* recommends that you ask yourself: [11]

Now, what to do?

When you see only one option, and it gets blocked, you feel trapped. You need to envision some alternatives. Stuck? Here's the easy way out. Get on the right path. The next time you're trying to figure out what route to take, expand your thinking and clear your head and try to answer these questions. [I've included my personal responses, but you should find your own answers.]

"Question 1: What matters most to you about this situation? " [11]

Answer 1: Try to get Jason to come over and break up with me in person, so I could find out why we were breaking up. I had so many questions and wanted to know if he still loved me.

"Question 2: What would you tell a friend to do in a similar situation?" [11]

Answer 2: Make an appointment to see a psychotherapist to help cope with my loss.

"Question 3: What else should you consider, in order to help you address the problem?" [11]

Answer 3: What are we going to do with the house if we don't get back together? Should I sell it, or buy him out? If Jason still loves me, should I ask him to go to counseling with me and try to work it out?

"Question 4: Envision yourself in each of your options. Which one feels best for you? Then you will get where you want to go." [11]

Answer 4: Be positive; to find out what is going on in Jason's head, get into counseling for myself to help cope with my loss. Try to get him to go to counseling and work things out, if he still loves me. If he is not willing to go, accept that the relationship is over. Get the house in my own name, and move on.

Answer 4 is exactly what I did.

Jason said he still loved me, but when it was his turn to see the psychotherapist, he didn't show up. So I asked him if I could buy him out, so I could keep the house.

He agreed, and now I live in my dream home all by myself. This is the first time in my life I have ever lived alone. I actually love it. I still have true happiness.

I went to counseling and my therapist helped me cope with my loss. She helped me find my inner child. She tried to help me cope with what my dad said to me about God and wanted me to start going to church again. But for a while, every time I went to the same church that my dad and I had gone to, I cried like a baby. Tears would be dripping out of my eyes. One time I went to church, a little girl looked at me as I was crying. She asked her mother, "Why is she crying?" It wasn't fair to the children to see me that way. Going to church is supposed to be a joyous time. My psychotherapist told me that I do belong there, and the more I go, the less I will cry.

I am finally able to go to church without it being just as painful to me as the first time I had gone. I will always love God.

She taught me how to date so that I won't end up with the same kind of man. She said that it's not a coincidence, but rather it is actually the attraction I have for these men and the attraction that they have for me because I was sexually abused.

She taught me about my depression. Last but not least, she taught me about drugs and alcohol so that I may be free from living with the addictions.

How do you think I should feel about the family member that sexually abused me? I have a good attitude about it. I hope he reads my book so he will know that I still love him with all my heart. I'm not sure why he did it, but I personally think someone did something to him. I know he feels bad about what happened between us, and I want him to know that I have sinned in my life too.

People have to forgive me for the things I have done wrong, just as I forgave him. We are all sinners. We are all God's children. We all deserve to find true happiness.

So, if you're not happy, find out why. Then do something about it, for true happiness is based on only three things:

Love

Wisdom

Forgiveness

May we all find true happiness!

Acknowledgements

1) *Playing It by Heart: Taking Care of Yourself No Matter What*
Melody Beattie
Hazelden Publishing: Foundation Center
Copyright 1999
"Light the flame inside your soul."

2) *The Nightmare Encyclopedia:Your Darkest Dreams Interpreted*
Jeff Belanger and Kirsten Dalley
New Page Books, A division of Career Press
Copyright 2006
Pages 5, 18, 19, 53, 189, 190, 256, 265, 266, 289, 290

3) *Want A Happier Life? Try This: A Gratitude Adjustment Is Simple Therapy*
Contributing Editor M. J. Ryan
Health Magazine
Copyright December, 2007
Page 74

4) *Christ Light* NTA & NTB Pre K-KNT2
Student Lessons 72N1211& 72N1221
Northwest Publishing House
Copyright 1998

5) *Codependent No More: How to Stop
Controlling Others and Start Caring For
Yourself*
Melody Beattie
Hazelden Publishing
Copyright 1986
Pages 18, 45, 54, 71, 103, 135, 136, 183,
216

6) *The Five Love Languages*
Dr. Gary Chapman
Moody Publishers
Copyright 1992

7) *Depression vs. Sadness / The Types of
Depression or Mood Disorders*
Dr. Charles E. Martin
http://www.clinical-
psychologist.com/depression.html
Copyright 2008

8) *Beyond Betrayal: Taking Charge of Your Life After Boyhood Sexual Abuse*
Richard B. Gartner
John Wiley & Sons Inc.
Copyright April 13, 2005

9) *The Power and Control Wheel*
Equality Wheels
Domestic Abuse Intervention Project
(Duluth)

10) *The Battered Woman*
Lenore E. Walker
Harper Collins Publishers
Pages 55 – 57
Copyright 1979

11) *Once Upon a Thigh*
Madison Women's Clinic
Copyright June 2007